Gerald's Journals:
The Life of an Everyday Hero

David
McElhinny

Armonia
Publishing

ISBN: 978-1-944613-00-6

Gerald's Journal is dedicated to my son,
Adam McElhinny, who makes this world a
better place just by being himself.

Sunday, September 10

I like writing because sometimes when I am at school and people are talking, a good idea comes to me that I could have said, but usually by then, whatever we are talking about is already over, so I don't say anything. When I am writing, I can take my time and say things just right.

I also really enjoy drawing. I like to draw pictures of my day.

I have school tomorrow and that makes me feel sad. I miss my friends

and teachers from my old school. So far at my new school I do not have friends. I also sit beside a boy named Nigel and he toots a lot and it smells like hard-boiled eggs that went bad.

Monday, September 11

I like Mrs. Watkins very much. She is a big, friendly lady who always wears bright clothes. Her eyebrows are funny looking because they look like they are drawn with pencils. She always smells like soap and when she talks her ears move and her earrings swing back and forth.

She is nice but I still do not like it when she comes to class because all of the other kids stare at me when she does. They know she is there to take me out of class to work on reading with her. She is the one who said I should start this journal because it will help my writing. I have been writing in it since the start of the year. She says I have a gift for writing. If that is true, then how come I have to go with her for reading instead of staying with my class? She said this journal is just for me and nobody else so I can write about anything I want.

Today we were working on present and past tense. That is a way to tell when something is happening. She has helped me a lot and I like her a lot. I just wish sometimes that other kids got pulled from class too.

On the bus today I saw a kid lick his finger and put it in another boy's ear. He yelled wet Willy. It was very gross.

Tuesday, September 12

This morning while my Dad was reading the newspaper, I snuck up on him and gave him a wet Willy. He was very surprised. Mom and Dad both laughed but then told me not to do it again. Especially at school! I always listen to my Mom and Dad so I won't do it ever again. I promised.

Last year at my old school the teachers were always happy with my schoolwork and all of the other kids were my friends. I was the best in the class at reading and math. Nobody told me that, but I just knew. I never said that I was the best because my Mom said that is called bragging and that is a bad thing to do because it can make other kids feel bad. I never want to make anybody else feel bad. I used to even get to help out some of the other kids sometimes. I liked that a lot and sometimes I used to think that maybe I would be a teacher when I grew up.

I sometimes wish I did not do so good at my old school because my parents said that I did so good that I needed to come to my new school now and I do not like it as good. Everybody always wanted to play with me at my old school.

I used to be the best in my class and now I am the worst. Instead of hearing "Great job Gerald" all the time like before, now all I ever hear is "No Gerald that is wrong. Try again." I do not want my Mom and Dad to feel bad about making me come here, so I do not talk about this to them.

I heard Mrs. Watkins tell my mom that I am very high functioning. Does that mean I am smart? I thought it did but I am not sure now.

Wednesday, September 13

Jimmy is always getting in trouble because he is a bad boy. He is bigger than everybody else and has mean eyes and big nostrils. A lot of days I can see the boogers in his nose. A lot of kids are afraid of him. His desk is in the corner of the room because he doesn't keep his hands to himself.

Today he played a mean trick on me. He was passing out gum to some of the other boys at recess. Recess is the only time we are allowed to have gum. He

saw me looking and walked over to me. He was smiling and being very nice. Usually he does not act that way. He offered me a piece of gum. I love gum. Everybody knows that I love to chew it and blow bubbles like my Dad showed me how. This gum was terrible. It was special gum that was made to be bad on purpose. It burned my ~~tonge~~ tongue and made me choke. My eyes watered and my nose was running. It tasted like fire. Jimmy and the other boys were pointing at me and laughing as I spit it out.

My Dad once said that nobody likes a ~~tattletail~~ tattletale so I did not tell on Jimmy. I never tell on him or the other boys when they are mean to me. Maybe I should.

Thursday, September 14,

   After school I was at speech therapy. I love to go there because Katie is very nice and always gives me a ring pop when we are done.

   She was telling my Mom how smart I am and how well I am doing. I wish the kids in my class would hear that. People like Katie are always telling my parents how well I do. They always seem so pleased with me and I like to go there because they make a big deal about me.

I do not have any friends from school that are my own age. Some of the older kids who live on my street are nice to me. I wish they were in my class because then I would have somebody to play tag with on the playground.

Sometimes Amanda and Graham come over and play in the sandbox with me. I love it when they do that because I can tell that my Mom

sometimes does not like to play in the sand. She does not like to get dirty but I do.

Sometimes in my room I like to pretend I am a super hero and I save the day. I get kind of sad when I realize that I am not a super hero but just a kid. If I was a super hero, maybe then I would have more friends at my new school.

Friday, September 15

Today was my day to be class leader. That means that I got to be first in line when we went to lunch, recess and gym. I also got to pass out the worksheets and take the ~~attention~~ attendance sheet to the office.

It was also my turn to bring something in for sharing. I brought my most favorite thing. It is an old saxophone that was given to me by my Dad. My Dad's best thing is piano. My Dad has been teaching me how to play both, but I like saxophone the best. Music comes much easier to me than schoolwork does.

I played part of a song at sharing and I think it surprised some of the other students that I was good. I usually make some mistakes but today I did not make any mess ups. I felt proud to show them that I could do that.

Liam and Rachel both told me that

I did a great job on the saxophone
and that they were impressed. They
still did not sit with me at lunch but
that is okay.

We had ice cream day in the
lunchroom and my Mom gave me an
extra 80 cents to buy a Chocotaco. I
think it is the best food ever made.

Today was a good day.

Saturday, September 16

I love Saturday because I get to spend the whole day with my Mom and Dad. They are a lot of fun. We went to the park today and we played tag. I love to play tag. Another boy joined in and played for a little bit but then he left.

We always go to Sweet Licks

after the park for ice cream. My Dad
always gets Moose Tracks. My Mom
got Pistachio ice cream today and my
Dad said it looked like ~~Leopardeon~~
Leprechaun poop.
It made Mommy
mad but I could
really tell that she
thought it was
funny too. Dad and
I laughed hard. I
always get vanilla
with sprinkles in a sugar cone because
it is the best. Tammy at Sweet Licks
always puts chocolate on it for eyes
and a mouth.

Sunday, September 17

Today was a great surprise. After church, we went home and changed our clothes. Daddy and Mommy said we were going on a drive. They tricked me, but in a good way, because instead we went down to Pittsburgh to watch the Pirates play against the Cardinals. We got to sit in a special box that was almost on the field. The Pirates beat the Cardinals 9 to 4. My Dad bought me wristbands. We always go to games early. My Dad says that is a great way to get balls. He was right.

Today after warmups, one of the

players ~~autograffed~~ autographed
a ball for me. Dad said the ball
is worth a lot
of money
now. Probably
about 10 million
dollars
I would
guess.

   After the game
we went to The
Pizza Place and ate pizza. Then I
climbed through the Playland. My
Mom and Dad climbed through a
couple of times, but my Dad said
his fat butt kept getting stuck. It
was funny.

I had a really fun day but I am still sad. That doesn't make sense I know. I do not like that the weekend is almost over and I have to go back to school.

Monday, September 18

In the morning time as the buses came in everybody was talking about what they did that weekend. As usual I sat at my desk working on the handwriting worksheets that Mrs. Baker gave me. I learned a long time ago when I was just a little kid that I have to work harder on some things than the other students.

Z in cursive is really hard to do and it looks strange to me.

Steven was walking around handing out invitations to his

birthday party to all of the boys in the class. Bobby was really excited because Steven said the party was at a club in the country that his family belongs to and there is an indoor pool with a slide. Mitchell said he has been there before and that it is really fun. Even Jimmy got invited and he is a bad boy.

I did not get invited. I know I am different in some ways, but really, I like all the same things as the other boys too. I love pizza, ice cream, swimming and recess, just like everybody else.

I pretended that I did not hear them talking about it. I wish I could go. It sounds like it will be fun.

Tuesday, September 19

Once a week I get pulled out of free reading time to go to the gymnasium for my gym class. This is one time that I do not mind leaving class. We get to play all kinds of fun games. There are five of us that do games, but today only four because Wesley was sick again and missed school. I hope he gets better soon.

Two boys don't talk at all. My mom says it is because they are ~~Artistic~~ Autistic. They are named Kurt and

Robbie and they like to play kickball and they are really good kickers.

Michael is a lot of fun. He tells everybody to just call him Wheels. That is because he has to use a wheelchair. He is great at relay races. He is so fast. I like Wheels a lot. He is very nice to me and always gives me a piece of butterscotch candy after class when Mr. Flukas is not looking. I think he is nice to me because he knows what it is like to be different.

Wednesday, September 20

Today on the bus Jimmy called me a retard. He said it to me real quiet, like he always does, so the bus driver did not hear. I know it is a bad word. I do not know what it

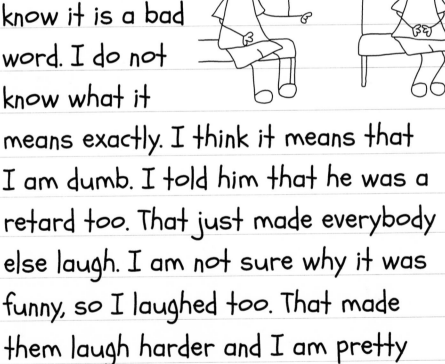

means exactly. I think it means that I am dumb. I told him that he was a retard too. That just made everybody else laugh. I am not sure why it was funny, so I laughed too. That made them laugh harder and I am pretty sure they were laughing at me. Being

mean back at him did not make me
feel better. It just made me feel
worse. I know I should not have said
that to him and maybe tomorrow I
will tell him I am sorry. I will never
use that word again.

Usually I try to sit in the front of
the bus because Jimmy and some of
the other not-so-nice boys sit in the
back. But today my math class with
Mrs. Watkins took long and I got to
the bus late.

Tonight was
spaghetti night
at home. It was
great.

Thursday, September 21

I am always the last one to get to lunch on Thursdays because of my reading class. Today we worked more on subject and predicate. These are the two parts of a sentence. The subject is what the sentence is about and the predicate tells something about the subject. I understood it well today.

I had to hurry up and grab my lunch box from the classroom and by the time I got there everybody was already eating.

A boy in third grade spilled his milk when Jimmy bumped into him. Jimmy did not even say he was sorry. That was wrong. I felt very, very, very bad for him.

My Mom always gives me two juice boxes because I like them a lot. I walked over to his table and he was trying not to cry. I gave him my juice box and he said thank

you. I think it made him happy to have something to drink. It made me happy to help him. Then I went back and sat at my regular table by the flag. I am most of the time the only one there.

My day turned bad after lunch. I got back to the classroom and Mrs. Baker said that she wanted to talk to me. She sent the other kids out to recess and then took me over to my desk. She made me look in my desk and I saw her Candy Apple with a couple big bites taken out of it. Rachel gave it to her in the morning and it was sitting on her desk all morning. She asked me why it was in my desk. Since I did not know why, I kept quiet. I had to spend recess inside today. That was a bummer. I think Mrs. Baker thinks that I took her candy apple.

Friday, September 22

The boy that I gave the juice box to smiled at me in the hall and waved hi. I said hi back to him but I do not know his name.

Jimmy got sent to the hall for making fart noises with his armpit. It was pretty funny but Mrs. Baker said he should not do that in class so he got in trouble. I waited to get home and then tried to do it but my armpit will not make that sound.

Mom and Dad took me to movie night at my school tonight. We

watched a cartoon and it was real funny
and exciting. We took sleeping bags
and sat on the gym floor to watch
the movie. My Mom brought popcorn
and root beer. I saw some of the kids
from my class there too. I did not talk
to them. I just sat and watched the
movie and had a good time.

Saturday, September 23

My mom is a great golfer. She played in college. She takes me to a small Par 3 course near our house to play when the weather is nice. She says I am a natural because of 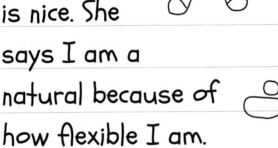 how flexible I am.

She said that being like me has some good things like me being super duper flexible. My Mom hits the ball really high and makes all of her putts. I mostly hit ground balls a lot.

But I did make one par today. That is the first time for me and I was very happy. I hit the ball from the tee and it went in the air and landed in front of the green. I then chipped it onto the green with my pitching wedge and it rolled close to the hole. Then I putted it in on my first try. Mom cheered loud and hugged me real hard.

Afterwards we had ~~Atalion~~ Italian ice. Mine was root beer flavored because I love root beer. Mom got lemon and I do not like it very much.

Sunday, September 24

Today my Dad and I built a fort in the woods behind my house. We used sticks and branches to make it. It took a long time but it was fun and worth it. My Dad put two big sticks 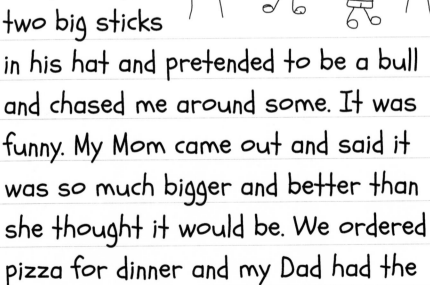 in his hat and pretended to be a bull and chased me around some. It was funny. My Mom came out and said it was so much bigger and better than she thought it would be. We ordered pizza for dinner and my Dad had the pizza guy deliver it to the backyard at our fort. The guy was cool and he pretended to knock on our fort door. My Dad gave the guy money. We ate the pizza inside. It was a great day.

Monday, September 25

    Today at school Mrs. Baker took me out in the hall and I thought I was in trouble again. She also made Jacob and Jimmy come into the hall too. She asked all three of us who stole her Candy Apple. I thought I was going to miss recess again. None of us said anything. Then she said

that one of the other students saw who took the Candy Apple and she wanted the truth. Jimmy asked who saw it but she would not say who.

Finally Mrs. Baker looked at Jacob and yelled "Spill it!" His face got red and he looked like he might cry. Then he said that him and Jimmy were the last ones in the classroom before lunch that day and that they took it and each took a bite. She asked how it ended up in my desk and Jacob said Jimmy put it in there. She was very mad and told them to tell me they were sorry. Jacob did but Jimmy would not say anything. His face was full of mad.

Mrs. Baker told me she was very sorry and that I should have told her it was not me that took it. She said that next time I need to speak up. I hope there is not a next time. Jimmy and Jacob both lost one week of recess. Jimmy said later in the day that he cannot believe they have to stay inside because of that dummy. He means me.

Tuesday, September 26

Today at sharing, Steven brought in his violin and played it for the class. I could tell that everybody thought it was terrible. It sounded like my cats when they fight. It was so ~~sqeeky~~ squeaky that some kids held their ears. I wanted to hold my ears too but I did not want to make him feel bad. But since this is just my journal for my eyes only I can say that he is very, very, very bad at violin.

Kiara has sharing next week and

47

she asked if she could bring in her bunny rabbit and Mrs. Baker said it would be okay because rabbits are quiet. Kiara said her mom would bring the bunny to school and then pick up the bunny at lunchtime but Mrs.

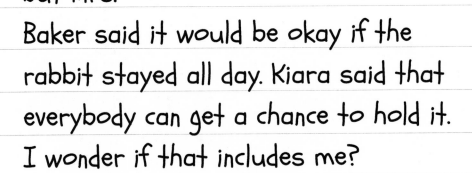

Baker said it would be okay if the rabbit stayed all day. Kiara said that everybody can get a chance to hold it. I wonder if that includes me?

Mrs. Baker told me that she wants for me to try to use contractions more often. That is when you take two words and make them into one. Like do not turns into don't and should not turns into shouldn't. I'll try to do that more from now on.

Wednesday, September 27

This morning on the school bus
a kid named Ryan puked all over the
floor and it smelled really, really bad.
As we went up and down the hills
the puke was sliding up and down the
floor. I kept my feet up on the seat
and so did the other kids. Ryan was
crying and I felt bad for him because

he was very sad. If he was not feeling good I wonder why he didn't stay home.

In class Mrs. Baker was teaching us about suffixes. She wrote some words on the board and told us to add the right suffix. One word was hop and Jimmy was called to the board and he wrote hoping. The teacher said that was not right. She called me next and I fixed it because it has two p's to make hopping. She

hopping

said good job. Now maybe Jimmy
won't think I'm not smart.

For the second day in a row my
Mom forgot to put a treat in my
lunch. She always gives me a creme-
filled cookie or cupcake. She never
forgets but did two times now. I'll try
to remember to ask her why.

Thursday, September 28

Jimmy had to go to the office today but I don't know why.

Today we got our spelling test back and I got all 20 right. Mrs. Baker put a big star on mine that said Terrific.

Mrs. Baker changed a rule today. For kids who carry their lunch to school we all used to have to line our lunch boxes or lunch bags on the shelf above where we hang our coats. But now we have to put them in a big, long file cabinet. When all the lunch boxes are in there now she locks it.

Gerald

Spelling
1 about
2 after
3 again
4 jump
5 keep
6 kind
7 think
8 those
9 three
10 step
11 scram
12 splat
13 craft
14 clam
15 grunt
16 brass
17 want
18 people
19 strap
20 sprint

TERRIFIC!

She unlocks it right before lunch and then we all can get them to take to the cafeteria. I wonder why that rule changed.

Friday, September 29

Today at recess I found a cool sports necklace in the grass. It is a special necklace that a lot of the boys wear because they say it makes you be better at sports. I asked my parents one time if I could have one but they said it is too expensive. I still wanted one and part of me wanted to keep the one I found.

But I know that is like stealing so I didn't keep it for myself even though I wanted to. I took the cool sports necklace to one of the teachers and she told me to take it inside to the office and I did. Mrs. Cratz is the school secretary and I told her I found the necklace and she took it and put it in the lost and found box. I like her a lot. She asked me how my Mom and Dad are doing and I told her fine.

When I was walking back down the hall to go outside for the last part of recess I decided to peek in the door to our classroom and I saw Jacob and Jimmy sitting there and they looked unhappy. Jacob didn't see me but Jimmy did and he waved one finger at me for some reason. I just turned away and went outside.

Saturday, September 30

Today I spent the day with Grammy
and Pappy.
Pappy took
me fishing
in the
afternoon.
We went
out on his pond in a little boat with
a little engine. He lets me run it and
steer it and I like it a lot. Pappy said
that worms work better but he
knows I don't like to hurt them so
we used ~~Saman~~ Salmon eggs instead.
Pappy caught two sunfish and one
catfish. I caught one sunfish and one
large mouth bass. Pappy said the

bass was the best fish of the day
and that they taste really good to
eat. We didn't eat them. We tossed
them back in the pond to catch
another day.

After dinner I helped Grammy bake
chocolate chip cookies and they were
really good. I ate five and Pappy said
he only had three but I counted that
he had seven. He fell asleep in his easy
chair and snored real loud.
Grammy and I laughed
and laughed.

Sunday, October 1

I love having sleepovers at Grammy and Pappy's house. I slept in my Dad's old room. When I woke up I could smell bacon cooking. Real bacon. At my house we always have turkey bacon because Mom says it's better for you.

Yum!

Yum!

At Grammy's we always have pig bacon and it tastes way better. I ate seven pieces of bacon, scrambled eggs and had chocolate milk and toast.

I went to their church with them.
It is a little different than my usual
church. At my church Pastor Herb
wears a suit, but at Pappy and
Grammy's church, the leader wears
a robe. I
sometimes
do not pay
attention at
church like
I should
because
I start
thinking about other things. But today
I heard a part where he said that
God created man in his own image. I
wonder if that includes me.

When we got back to their house,
Pappy took me for a ride on his old
tractor and then we played Frisbee
and then watched some TV until
Mom and Dad came and got me. I
was happy to see them but sad too
because I knew the weekend was over
almost.

Monday, October 2

Today at lunch a kid who I don't know came over to my table and said thank you for finding his cool sports necklace and turning it in to the lost and found. I told him he was welcome. He was wearing his cool sports necklace. He said it fell off at recess but he didn't even know it was missing until later. He said it was a birthday gift and that he felt happy to have it back.

Today Mrs. Baker wrote XX on the board and asked anybody if we knew what it said. Jimmy shouted out that it was a certain kind of movie. Mrs. Baker got mad at him and told him to go sit in the hall. XX is Roman for the number 20. I remember seeing some X's on the Grandfather clock at my Pappy and Grammy's house. A Grandfather clock doesn't have numbers. So far I know that I is 1, X is 10, XX is 20 and V is 5.

Tuesday, October 3

Big news today. Huge news. I was in music class when I had to get the hall pass. I was in the bathroom when the fire alarm went off. I wasn't done yet. It took me a couple minutes to finish. I have to make number two in school a lot because my Mom makes me drink prune juice every morning. She says it will make me regular. It never does. It just makes me poop. When I finished, I walked into the hall because the rule is to walk instead of run during fire drills. But this was not a drill. When I got into the hall there was smoke. There was nobody in the hall or in the classrooms. I was scared but tried to be calm as I walked fast to the doors. But then I remembered about Floppy. Today was Kiara's turn for sharing and she brought in her pet bunny. His name is Floppy and after sharing she put him in a cage in the back of the room and he was real quiet.

I went into our classroom. Nobody had been there because they were all at music. All but Mrs. Baker. When we have a special, she goes to the teacher lounge and after she comes back her breath smells like coffee. I could not believe it when I walked into the room. The rug on the floor that we use for circle time was on

fire. It is lucky that Mrs. Baker is
teaching us about plants because she
keeps a big water jug on her desk
to water the plants by the window.
I grabbed the jug and dumped it on
the fire and put it out. There was so
much smoke that it was choking me
and burning my eyes.

I went to the back of the room

and picked Floppy out of his cage. I was afraid because he looked dead. I decided to break the rules for the first time this year and I held Floppy in my arms and ran out of the room and down the hall to the outside doors.

When I came outside, all the kids were in the fire drill lines on the playground cement. I stopped running and I walked to my line with my class. Mrs. Baker came running to me and hugged me in her arms. Then Kiara ran to me and I handed Floppy to her. His nose started to twitch and he started to look okay again. I told Mrs. Baker that I was in the bathroom when I heard the fire alarm and that I came out as quick as I could. I told her that I remembered Floppy and knew I better get him too. I thought I was going to be in trouble but Mrs. Baker hugged me again and then I knew I wasn't in trouble. I told her about the fire in her room and how I dumped water on it. She hugged me even more.

The firemen came in three big red

trucks. Since it was afternoon anyhow, we just spent the rest of the day outside playing and then got on the buses and went home for the day.

Wednesday, October 4,

When I got to school today I found out that Jimmy can't go to our school anymore. Yesterday when we had music, he took the other hall pass after I left and said he had to go to the bathroom too. I didn't see him in the bathroom. That's because he didn't go there. He had a lighter and a bunch of smoke bombs. He ran down the hall lighting and throwing them. That's why there was so much smoke. He tossed one of the smoke bombs into our empty classroom. The door was open because we didn't have class at that time and that is the rule. The smoke bomb made the rug catch on fire. After he threw the smoke bombs he went back to the class and sat down. I heard one of the other kids say that as soon as Jimmy got back the alarm went off. Mr. O. talked to the principal about it because Jimmy gets in trouble a lot.

They checked his locker and found more smoke bombs and that is how they caught him. I feel bad for him because he doesn't have

a Mom or Dad and he lives with his
aunt instead. I hope he is okay.

At lunch today I sat at my regular
table by myself. Then Kiara, Megan
and John came over and asked if they
could sit with me and I said yes. Kiara
gave me brownies that she said she
made with her mom to give to me. I
sometimes am worried when people
act nice that they are tricking me. I
decided to trust her and I am glad I

did because the brownies were great!
There were eight of them all for me.
I decided to share them with Kiara,
John and Megan so we each got two
and that made us all happy.

Kiara said they took Floppy to the
bunny doctor and that he was going
to be okay. She said the doctor said
that the reason Floppy was sleeping
and looked dead was because the
smoke got into his lungs. He told
her that a couple more minutes
and Floppy could have died and that
I saved his life. That made me feel
proud.

John told me again he thought
I was great on the saxophone. We

talked a lot and it was the best lunch all year because I had people who wanted to talk to me.

When I got home from school, a man stopped by the house to take my picture and ask me some questions. My Mom says he is from the newspaper and that people need to hear the story about what happened at school yesterday. I told him everything I could remember, but my Mom told me to leave out the part about how prune juice makes me have to go poop a lot.

Thursday, October 5

Today I got invited to Mark's birthday party. He passed out invites to every boy in the class. Even me. It is another swimming party. He asked me if I knew how to swim and I said yes I learned when I was eight. This time it is at his house. He said he has a heated pool and he said there would be pizza too. I can't wait. I told Mom that we had to go get a present for him but she said the party isn't for two weeks so we have plenty of time to find just the right gift. Mark likes soccer so I was thinking about a soccer ball.

At lunch today my table was full of kids from my class. There were so many that they had to squeeze in. The rule is that only eight kids can sit at one table together but we had eleven and I couldn't believe the mean lunch lady with the net in her hair and the black thing on her lip didn't yell at us. It was fun and we laughed a lot. Russell told a funny joke. Knock Knock. Who's there? Ivana. Ivana Who? Ivana kiss you and then he pretended that he was going to kiss Rachel who screamed and almost fell out of her chair. I laughed very hard.

At recess I got asked to play freeze tag for the first time all year and it was very fun. We played for the whole recess. One time four kids were frozen and I ran all the way around a big tree and came up behind them and made them unfrozen. When

I was frozen once, Jacob unfroze
me. I didn't think he liked me but he
tagged me and said come on Gerald,
run fast and I did.

My Mom and Dad took me out to
dinner at my favorite pizza place and
it was great. When we got there we
got a nice surprise because Kiara and
her Mom and Dad were there too. It
was great to have somebody to talk
to while the grownups did grownup
talk. This pizza place has crayons
on the table and you are allowed
to draw all over the table because
the top is made of paper. I drew a
house with smoke coming out of
the ~~chim knee~~ chimney. Kiara drew a

picture of me and her holding hands with Floppy and smiling.

Kiara's Dad told me that I am Floppy's guardian angel.

Friday, October 6

This has been the best week ever.
Today we had an assembly. It was not
on the schedule so it was a surprise
to everybody. When we found out all
the kids cheered in class because that
means no class during the assembly
time. We all went to the
~~additorium~~ auditorium and
sat in our lines.
Three big men
came out on
stage with a
spotty dog.
They were
firemen and
they gave us

a lesson on fire safety. I remembered one of them from the other day when they came to my school. We learned stop, drop and roll. They got a third grade kid on stage and put him in a full fireman uniform that was too big. He looked funny and almost fell when he tried to walk.

At the end of the assembly they said they had a surprise. They were giving an award out. When they called my name I didn't know what to do. Jacob and Russell told me to stand up and I did. The fireman asked me to come up on stage with him and I did. The fireman told the whole school the story about me saving Floppy

and how I used my noodle to put out
a fire. He made a mistake because
I used the water jug, not a noodle,
but I didn't say anything about his
mistake because I didn't want him to
feel bad.

Then they gave me an official
fireman hat, a fireman badge and
a big, shiny gold medal that they
put around my neck. When they did
this the whole school stood up and
cheered really loud for me. Then all
the kids yelled my name over and over.
Gerald! Gerald! Gerald! The medal said
Bravery on it. The spotty dog then
kissed me on the mouth with a big
lick. I wasn't ready for that and my

mouth was part way open so it was really gross because I felt his wet tongue on my teeth.

When I looked out from the stage I saw my Mom, Dad, Pappy and Grammy standing in the back. I didn't know they were there. Mom and Dad were crying but I could tell they were crying because they were happy for me.

Now I have a lot of friends.
Everybody talks to me in the halls
and plays with me at recess and sits
with me at lunch. Most of the time
I hated coming to school but now I
love coming. It's fun and I have lots
of good friends now.

   I am a lucky boy!

About the Author

David McElhinny is an award-winning
sports columnist, editor and author.
He lives in Mars, Pennsylvania with his wife,
Bonnie, and sons, Sean and Adam.

CPSIA information can be obtained at www.ICGtesting.com
Printed in the USA
LVOW08s0153030816

498821LV00001B/127/P